A,B,C BOOK OF INSPIRATIONAL POETRY

FOR EVERYDAY LIFE AND EMOTIONS

ISBN-10: 978-1-7358756-2-0

LOC#: 2020917986

Publisher, Editor and Graphics:

Fiery Beacon Publishing House, LLC

(Fiery Beacon Consulting and Publishing Group)

Greensboro, N.C.

Printed in the United States of America.

A, B, C

BOOK OF INSPIRATIONAL POETRY FOR EVERYDAY LIFE AND EMOTIONS

BY

AUTHORESS CARLA BLAKE

Table of Contents

U

Acknowledgements

First, I have to give thanks to my Heavenly Father; He is the reason for all my blessings.

My journey so far, has been very extraordinary to say the least.

The chapters in my book called life get bigger and better. While I am going through these chapters, I tell myself I must remain humble, loving, and at peace and most importantly, never forget where I emerged from.

I also want to thank my loving family and friends. They have helped me through the dark nights and through the blissful walks through the gardens.

No matter where I may walk on my path of life, I know my God will follow me.

He will never leave me nor forsake me.

Thank you to all my readers, those who I have met and have yet to meet. I love you all and thank you for your support.

Be blessed,

#C.M.B Christ Made Believer

Aspirations

What are your aspirations in life?

Do you dream of things that are not?

What keeps you driven and focus on not losing?

Aspirations should be thought out clearly

Thought out for success

With intentions of completing

Aspirations should be positive

Uplifting and personally rewarding

They are what keep you going

And your mind focused

There are plenty of paths

You just have to choose it

And own it

Don't let your aspirations

Become fallen and forgotten

Keep pushing

The finish line isn't much further

Abandonment

Lost and helpless

Are the only words that find me

Wishing for hope

To surround me

No strings attached

Yes I said that

No strings pulling me up

From this hole of emptiness

Surrounded and enclosed

No way to get out

Won't someone please

Help me out!

I'm just trying to get

out! Find the light

Is it just me?

Or is it too much to ask?

People gave up on me

That was hard to grasp

Especially when you have nothing left

I just want to be free

Free from the worldly chains holding me

Once I am free

My heart will truly sing!

Broken

I was once broken

And was in a place of deep loss

I retreated my mind

And left my thoughts

Trying to piece together

Who I once was

So I searched for that person

I knew I was

Fixing the puzzle

Can be difficult sometimes

Especially when those pieces

Are hard to find

I'm a diamond in the rough

Buffed and shined

I shine bright

Even in the midst of dark times Brokenness can
be mended

It can be healed

Keep searching my friend

The pieces will be revealed

Brotherly Love

Why is there so much hate

In the world nowadays

In the Bible

It says we must love and pray

Show love amongst your brethren

Don't leave them stranded

As the parable portrays it

We must treat each other

As we ourselves would want to be treated

Yet the argument

Often gets heated

My brother or sister

Doesn't have to be blood

It's the genuinity of the heart

That means the most

Share and love

Spread the love God shows us

For it is Him we should show

The same likeness thereof

Change Your Mindset – Change Your Results

The change in you

Starts within your mind

Believe in your heart

And you will find

The power in you

Is greater than you could imagine

Because faith starts small

And miracles can happen

Your days ahead

Are full of endless possibilities

Nothing can stop you

Not even your enemies

Keep God by your side

You will not fail

The tribulations ahead will not succeed

You will prevail

Keep pushing

Keep fighting

This is not the end

Your days ahead

Will be full of longevity and happiness

Confusion

I am so confused

About life and all its qualities

Why is there evil in the world

And no equality

Waking up each morning

Starting on my way

Not knowing

What could happen today

But I remain confident

And just pray

Each and everyday

That the devil won't confuse me

Or come my way

Why are there murders

And robberies

Child abuse

And mass shootings?

Where is the love

That feels the air

Is it all gone?

Has it all disappeared?

What about the White House?

Why can't they agree?

All the bickering and rumors

Have to cease

What about the police

And the brutality

Senseless beatings

And killings

But I know it's all things of the earth

That started from the beginning

When man was first birthed

But if we all stand together

Hand in hand

We can bring all this nonsense

To an end

Decisions

Sometimes I don't know what to do

What to say

Or what to feel

I don't know what to think

Or whether I should believe

The things that I am hearing

It's like looking through a cloud

I can't see things clearly

Decisions can be hard

Some may be easy

But some never come quickly

When I don't have the answers

I always pray

That my Heavenly Father will show me the way

He hears my cries

When I'm in distress

When I can't tell my right from my left

I worry each day

That the decisions I make

Be strong and not break

When I'm stuck at the crossroads

Of life

And it seems the world is against me

I have no reason to fear

For my God is with thee

He will never leave me nor forsake me

Encouragement

When you feel like giving up

And it seems like all your hope is gone

Don't give up

Just hold on

Lift yourself up

Don't look down

You can't start your day off

With a frown

Speak to your inner self

Down to your soul

Shake your spirit up

Stand tall and be bold!

People will doubt you

And leave you hanging dry

But remember some people are just meant to be

In your life for a short time

Stay focused

Be positive

Keep the energy

Flowing through your heart

God has too much

In store for your life

So why give up now?

Be proud, stay encouraged

Keep being you

The best thing to do

Is to stay true

Expectations

We start each day

Always expecting something

Whether it is from others

Or simply ourselves

And if our expectations

Are not met or followed

We tend to lose ourselves

You can't always depend

On the ways of others

Because you might be disappointed

By what you see

But your expectations

From the one up high

Will never fail or lie

We can't expect others

To please us

Because they are just as us

Human creatures

We make mistakes

We lose our temper

We cry and laugh

It's a constant cycle

Expect more out of yourself

Set your standards high

Start today

Time is wasting by

Faith

You are the reason I live

The air I breathe

You're my hope for tomorrow

The light that shines in the dark tunnel

The push I need to go on

When I'm at my lowest

The reason you care so much

Is because I am your chosen

My faith in you will never die

My belief in you is strong

Whenever I try to leave

You keep holding on

My spirit is awakened

When I speak to you

You know me inside and out

Up to the highest altitude

When all goes wrong

In this life around me

My faith in you will stand strong

I am nothing without you

Gratitude

To you I show my gratitude

My love, my heart

Is all I can give you

When I have nothing to give

I can fill that emptiness

With all the love I have

Thank you for who You are

I may not say that enough

But I mean it

From the bottom of my soul

I can't thank You enough

For the things You've done

I didn't deserve them

That's for sure

Lord I love You

I give You all the praise

I will forever follow You

I will never stray

Grace

Why must I trust you?

Why should I throw the towel in?

I feel like giving up

I'm at my weakest

What do you have to offer

I have nothing to give

So why do you keep sending

Your rescue ship

I see you coming

You're getting close

But I keep swimming away

I don't want to come ashore

But I'm still floating

I think I'm going to make it

I see something ahead

With my name written on it

What I see

Is Your infinite grace

And it's right there

For me to take

It's Your gift to me

And You sent your Son down

To save me

I trust you Lord

With all of me

I humble myself

So You'll be proud of me

No matter what situation I'm in

I know You'll fix it

It doesn't matter how

I will have faith and receive it

Hurt

I know You see the pain in my eyes

The pain I try to hide

Each and every day

I tell myself I will survive

For God said He will not put more on me than I can bear

That is true, I can tell

Because I know He loves me

My future looks bright you see

All the things He has planned for me

Are lined up on the path to my destiny

My future is filled with amazing stories

That's why the devil keeps coming for me

I have the devil shook

He doesn't know what to think

Because the path of destruction he lined up for me

Won't succeed

I climbed mountains

As you can tell

My faith surpasses

The many hopeless eyes that look down on me

But only if they knew

The amazing wonder they stare upon

My name will forever live on and on.....

Hope

I hope and pray one day, that things won't be the same

I hope and pray one day, that those around me

Will change their ways

I start to think in my mind

That I'm on my own

I cannot do it

I'm only me

I need the strength of Jesus

He will do it

He can fix it

I know He can

All this turmoil we live in

I hope our children pray

I hope they find their way

I pray they don't make our mistakes

Our children are our tomorrow

My hope for them

Is to ensure no sorrow

But days filled with bliss

They won t have to borrow

Infinite

We live in a world

Where there are infinite things

Things that last forever in our dreams

But waste away in reality

Infinity means endless

It continues to go on

But life isn't that way

It can be cut off short

You must live your days

As if they're your last

Living your life to the fullest

You couldn't go wrong with that

Be wise about your choices

Mistakes lurk not far away

You can't erase the past

Its etched permanently in your brain

Infinity moves forward

It creates more space

It opens your mind

To ideas and traits

Don't get lost in the openness

Soak it all in

The world is yours

To bask in

Keep moving forward

Be proud of who you are

There is no one else like you

You're the twinkle in the star!

Just In Case

Just in case things

Don't go my way

I have to remember

That there is God's way

My life won't always

Be on track

I may stumble off

And think I know the facts

No worries

I know if I lose my way

The light God shines upon me

Will find its way

No matter how far I stray

I can come back

Things will get better

I know that

So just in case

People let me down

I won't worry

My smile is my crown

God is my king

My best friend indeed

If all fails

I know I have Him beside me

Judgment

We should not judge others

For we don't know where they came from

Let him without any sin

Cast the first stone

We should treat others

As we would want to be treated

Because in God's eyes

We are all equal

Why criticize others

For things you've also done

Why must you point fingers?

You are not the judge

We all face trials

And situations

That place us in

predicaments

We don't wish to be in

Just ive your life

Anc yours only

It's your path

You have the ability to choose it

Knots and Tangles

Sometimes the thoughts

In my mind

And the words that come from my lips

Get tangled

It frustrates me

Because I sometimes can't get the right angle

My mind is always going

Like the wind that blows for miles

It's always reaching a new destination

Meeting new smiles

The imagination and beautiful ideas

God has instilled inside my mind

Reach depths

No man has known

I open my mind

Each day, more and more

That way God can place

More knowledge inside me

And allow my thoughts to grow

Love

Love is patient

Love is kind

Love makes the universe entwine

It's beautiful

It's brave

It doesn't make mistakes

Sweet as a baby cheeks

And sour as spoiled milk

Smooth as silk

And hard as rusted nails

It's hard work

It takes some time

It won't be perfect all the time

But you keep pushing

Keep fighting

It's all worth it in the end

Love doesn't judge

It never lies

It will never leave you

Never says goodbye

Each one of us are special

Unique

But love is a part of each of us

It runs heart deep

Despite all the differences

It's what makes us all the same

It connects us

It's surreal

No playing games

But if we could just use a little more

Give a little more

Things might be different

Could you imagine a world

With no violence or no evil?

Everyone together

No separation

But unity and a peaceful nation

That's the main goal

To all be equal

One nation

One people

Misunderstood

I feel like no one understands me

They don't understand me

I feel like I'm speaking through a megaphone

With no sound leaving

My words break apart

And are left unheard

Why must I be

So misunderstood

Why must I be "like" them?

Why must I change?

Why must I adapt?

Just to be equal

In this moment I'm me

And in this moment, I'm free

Free to make my own decisions

And do me

I'm a strong, independent being

Placing my stamp on the earth

I'm doing things God's way

For He's the source of all my blessings and returns

For being misunderstood

Means others simply can't relate

I was meant to be different

I was cut from a different kind of cloth - period

Noise

My thoughts and sight

Sometimes feel crowded

The noise in my ears is loud

My vision blurry and obstructed

I used to wonder

What it was

Was it the devil

Trying to create a distracting image?

But in later time

I knew what it was

God sending me signals

So I would be alert

I cleared my thoughts

And the clutter

God then revealed to me

My purpose

He showed me the world

He opened and paved the way

For me to go forth

There are doors ready for me to open

And I have the key

To the world He holds before me

Natural

I know some things seem unexpected

But really some are just natural

Everything on this earth

Has a time and place

A time to be birthed

And a time to be erased

Some things seem second nature

Not first come

I wish sometimes

They were though

But everything is in God's plan

That's the plan I should follow

But sometimes I let my "natural" self

Chew more than I can swallow

Just wait and listen

Hear what the Lord has to say

For His words are life

In dark places

Naturally we get impatient

And decide to jump the gate

But as natural beings

We must appreciate

The one they call great!

For He is everything we anticipate and more

Obstacles

What is an obstacle? A

stumbling block

That stops us?

Obstacles diverts us and move us out the way

Some are temporary and some are permanent

Just make sure the (destruction) doesn't stay

Just move on

Change your pathway

We all make mistakes

Were all human

No one is perfect

Not even those who assume it

I used to let obstacles Put

me at a halt

Standby....

Time would seem to fly by

Now I face them head on

It's a challenge

But I know God is standing on the sidelines

Open arms with love and anticipation

As sure as the flowers bloom

In May

I know God favors me

Because the rays of sunshine parade on me

Obsession

We've become so attached

To the things of this world

We tend to lose our head

All trying to be the same

Because we're obsessed

Obsessed with society

And their ways

No one wants to be different

Being unique

Is thrown out the window

And into the street

Obsessed with new traditions

And standards

We shouldn't have to adapt

To this generation's methods

Old tricks

And wise words

Can still be applied

The wisdom from our forefathers

Is what will help us survive

Don't be envious

And want what others have

The grass isn't always greener on the other patch

Enjoy what's yours

You may not get it back

Our days are numbered

Be grateful for what you still have left

Prayer

My prayer to you

Is one that's simple

Not repetitive

Not evil

I want you to hear me

The things I have to say

The expressions in my heart

I don't know how to say

For my words to you

Are special

Almost like

A sweet smelling perfume

I want to connect with You

Become a part of You

Feel You

When I pray I hope my words reach You

And serenade You

Like the sound of music

Hear me oh Lord!

I wish to seek you

To be in your presence

Is what I long for

Preparation

I must always be prepared

For life's constant changes

For things are always changing

Things never remain the same

They aren't meant to remain

For things grow old

And wither away

Always be prepared

You never know what will come your way

No matter the test or trial

My God will find a way

During the wait period

I must be patient

For God is bringing me out of the ditch

And towards my destination

Keep living life intentional

And be willing to change

Stay humble and loving

And your peace shall remain

God hears my plea

He answers my calls

His plan for me

Will always come out on top

A Time To Be "Quiet"

There is a time to speak

And a time to not speak

Sometimes our words

"In the moment"

Can be miss perceived

So, we have to choose wisely

And think before we speak

Words can be like a two-edged sword

They can cut deep

Rest and let your heart speak

It knows you better than you think

That situation you been battling

Those few words you wanted to say

Leave them alone

God will put His "2 cents" in

Hush, don't speak

Let your mind retreat

In the end

It will create peace

Quietness

Be quiet

And listen

You can hear the words of the Lord

When you move to quickly

You may miss some instructions

It's important to find your place

A place of quiet and serenity

For in this place

Is where you meet your inner being

In your quiet space

Love yourself

Applaud yourself

You've come a long way

Now walk amongst this Earth

With confidence and a smile on your face Your amazing

You wo(man) of God

The way you carry yourself

Is a million to one

Your humble spirit

Carries many

So keep that pace

It will be rewarding!

Respect

Love thy neighbor

Creature of the earth

Treat those around you

As you would yourself

Be kind and remain humble

Because what's yours now

Could be someone else's tomorrow

If someone may treat you unfairly

Or throw dirt on your name

Don't fall to their level

Because the regret will carry shame

Lead by example

There are always eyes watching

Do the right thing

For the glory will be amazing

Return and Rewards

I know that which was taken from me

Removed or stolen

Will be return to me without void

That which was once void

Is now approved

Accepted

And received

I have conquered

That which was once a "hill"

The pit which I was once in

I have prevailed

Wrongs have been made right

I have been rewarded for my faithfulness

I am amazing

The things I can do are endless

Nothing can stop me

When the ball in my court is rolling

When I have God on my side

Nothing's impossible......

Everything just keeps going

Strength

Give me your strength

Lord I can't go on

If I lose Your grasp

I know I can't go on

Stay with me

Keep me warm in your arms

When I fall Lord

Lift me up!

Thank You Lord

For being my strong tower

When there is nothing

But shambles around me

When there is nothing but evil around me

When there is stress filled days

Lord surround me

I know that feeling

Yes I do

That feeling of peace and serenity

I know that's You

Telling me things will get easier

Everything will be okay

Because you are my refuge

My angel awaiting

Statue Position

We experience situations

That we feel as if we're stuck in

As If were a cement image

Sometimes we get stuck there

Grounded and locked

We form our lives

Around the things that seem to go on

Earthly things don't last

And they don't matter

Their equivalent

Is like that of dirt scattered

Don't get stuck

In the afflictions that follow you

They may attack you

But they cannot break you

Hold strong to your faith

And listen to God

Because His ways are righteous

They are never wrong

Move and don't wait

Tomorrow isn't promised

Believe and you shall find

Your destined promise

Silently Moving

Patiently I'm waiting

For my God to reply

But I'm still silently moving

Just as clouds pass by

He said work

While you wait

Don't waste time

For you never know

When He'll arrive

Serve

And your happiness will come

While helping others

Is when you truly have won

I know you wonder

When your day will come

For victories and blessings

Will be more than one

Be proud of where you are

He knows where you came from

Just sit back and wait

For your glory days to come

Thankful

Lord I thank you

For everything

The little

And the big

The things I can't see yet

I have to believe

They've already been created

The behind the scene events

And the battles that I've overcome

I have you to thank

You're the reason I breathe

The reason I wake up

You're my personal coach

And the one who cheers me up

Thank You for believing in me

When my hopes were lost

You renewed my strength

Wher I had none

I need You now

And forever

With You

I'll see no failure

The elevation of my life

Is quickly moving

Things are moving in the right direction

And they are going smoothly

Greatness doesn't stop here

It keeps going.....

My destiny is already in place

Because in my dreams

You already showed me

Time

Why does it seem like I'm going in circles?

I take one step forward

And two steps backwards

I keep rushing and not thinking

Wishing things would go my way

But I'm on God's timing

Things must go His way

I can't comprehend the reason why

I'm not where I should be in my life

But maybe I am

Right where God wants me

Aligned with my purpose - exactly

Things may not

Make sense now

But in the end

I know I'll be proud

Proud of where I came from

And who I've become

Everyone will be amazed

To see my outcome

Unfeigned Faith

Door on hinges

Can be moved

But not my faith

It won't be "Whoo'd"

People will tempt you

Things will haunt you

Sometimes life

Will taunt you

But keep pushing my friend

Things get better

Keep your head up

And ride the stormy weather

The waves will cease

And the sun will appear

The clouds will burst into cheers

It's a sign

That things do get better

You've got to keep your faith

And pray for better

Undeniable Truths

I cannot deny

The simple facts and truths

The fact that I'm amazing

And beautiful

My humble spirit

Gets me through

And my calm demeanor

Brings much blessing and truth

I cannot deny

The love You have for me

It is like no other

You show me grace and favor time and time again

My belief in Your results

Will never waiver or end

The motion in life continues to roll

When You are present

Is when things start going forward

That's when I realized

Your name

Is the one I got to mention

I can't go another day

Without acknowledging You

Or showing You my love

Because You never miss a day

Showing me Your love

Vast Majority

I may be accepted by a few or even many

Here on this Earth

But I know up above in thy heavenly kingdom

I'm accepted without a doubt

The heavenly angels adore me

God loves me

I'm a star in their eyes

Surpassing the amazing

My story is like none of the rest

The details are intriguing

And once it ends

I'll go down in history

I'm not like the majority

I'm quite different you see

My name rings different

When people speak it

My name has a story to tell

The cracks in the seams of my book

Are proof I've had failures

Don't worry

I've had many victories too

For these pages are proof

Of my testimonies and truths

Views From Afar

What beauty

The views I see

The streets and blocks

Connect and form a mystery

To a new dimension

One we've yet to see

It makes you wonder

The stories it has to speak

Traveling a long way from home

There's no place like home

But my eyes have yet to see

All things God has in store for me

I pray God takes me far

Very far

So I can view things from a different point

And kiss the stars

I see and feel

The presence of God around me

That's how I know

He still holds his promise

I'm ready to board

This ship and sail

Across the waters of life

Just as a dove drifts without a care

What's Next?

Deep thoughts

Words randomly appearing at night

As I lay awake dreaming

I wonder about my future

Interactions and businesses

And how many I'll be seeing

Will I'll be able to leave a mark

In my community, streets and children

I can do more

I can go higher

The restless nights

Will soon show their price

I'm not finished

I'll be up next

My turn is around the corner

One block ahead

I will keep pushing

I can't stop

Because giving up

Means I might lose my spot

"What's next they say?"

I say I AM

Here I AM

Now watch me take a stand

Worth It

The price You paid

For me

Makes my life seem

Undeserving

The life You built for me

It makes it all worth it

You gave me life and air

In my body and lungs

So I breathe

And sing praises and songs

The people and places

You've allowed me to be upon

Are blessings in disguise

Every single one

Every mistake and every lesson

Taught me something

That my life is important

And well worth it

The beautiful presence before me

Means it's all true

That miracles and dreams can come true

All of this is worth it;

The hard work

The pain

The confusion

The bliss

The blessings

And opportunities

It's all for You Lord

I owe it all to You

Xcellence Does Exist

I am "xcellent"

I am amazing

I'm a strong woman

Living amongst God's presence

I'm in awe of Your glory

The beauty around me is astonishing

Even though I depart from one place

You follow me always

This world isn't perfect

And neither am I

But with my "xcellence"

I can make it a little bit more brighter

I believe I am the key

To set some things free

I will make things happen

Because I have "xcellent" blood in me

I am "xcellent" indeed

Yes I am

God made me special

I shall fulfill who I am

"X" Marks The Spot

X

Marks the territory that I'm on

The ground I'm on shakes

When I step on

Because I walk in confidence and peace

Knowing my battles are won

I define all odds set up against me

Or to attack me

I won't lose

Because my God walks beside me

X means no limitations

It doesn't stop here

It marks my destination

Where I'm reaching towards

The prize lies within me

The search ends here

X is me

I'm the final piece

I'm what they've been looking for

So here I am

All of me

Here to bless your presence

And the world around me

Be The You Inside Of Yourself

Always keep you in mind

Best interests only

Negative thoughts

Won't help anyone or anything

Just the society that yearns for it

Never feed into its traps

Once your inside

It's hard to get out

The world can either be an endless hole you fall straight into

Or an endless hill of possibilities

That will continue to enlighten you

Let the hills roll in your life

Let the doors of possibilities stay open

If they shut

That means your belief wouldn't keep them open People
will judge you

100

Talk about you

And dislike you

But does that mean what they say is true?

You have nothing to prove

Be yourself

Don't change one thing

Be the (Queen/King) you were destined to be

Yearly Yearnings

Day in and day out

We yearn for more

For something different

Things we can't "afford"

Yearning for materials

And things we don't have

Envying the lives

We don't have

Yet I yearn for something different

The love of my Father God

To live a life pleasing in his sight

To be accepted by heavenly angels

And walk with them side by side

Yearnings can feel like an eternity

Because the things we want most

Seem to not come

But everything we don't have

We don't always need to have fulfillment of

We should just live life

As God intended for it to be

Happy and free

And filled with love and peace

Zoom In And Focus

Just zoom in and focus

That drama around you is bogus

Don't let it affect you

Keep riding and stay driven

You're a star, you always have been

Keep gleaming

Stay focused on you

Remove your lens

In this season you can't be covered

You can't block the things within

Let everything out

Stand on the rooftops and shout

Because the devil is lurking

And seeking you out

God said,

"The plans I have for you"

"To prosper and not leave you"

This year will be my reward

If I stay determined and consistent

New and better things will come

The rest of my days will be victorious

Zealous Spirit

My heart leaps

And my soul is filled with joy

Every time I think

Or hear Your name

When I speak Your name

It seems as though

The world around me

Stops moving

As the worries and troubles in my life

Fade away

The warmth of Your love

Overpowers

And takes over

The sweet words you speak to me

Are like music

My mind dances

To the rhythm

I yearn to be close

Closer to you each day

Whenever I stray

To be closer to you again, is the words I pray

My name is Carla Marie Blake and I am twenty-seven years old. I currently reside in South Carolina.

I have found my purpose in life as a writer and I enjoy writing whole heartedly. It is not only a passion of mine, but a gift. The book you hold before you was written in some of my darkest moments along with my greatest.

These poems, or as i would like to call them letters, to you are all very true. Each was

derived from an emotion or moment that took place in my life. I believe God took me through these events so I could release my thoughts into a beautiful passage. As you read the letters on these pages, I pray that they resonate with you and bring joy and peace to your heart. Please enjoy these words from spirit that I have created for you

#C.M.B #Christ Made Believer

Order my book, **Learning Through Poetry The Bible Vol. 1**

Buy on Amazon or email me at carlablake11@gmail.com

Follow me on social media:

Facebook: Carla Blake (Author page @Authoress Carla Blake)

Instagram: @Carlamb12

Thank you so much for your support!

Stay tuned for more books coming to a store near you!